Stockholm 1
Guide 2023

The thorough travel guidebook provides information, maps, and suggestions for an enjoyable and easy vacation.

Violet M. Schulze

Table of contents

WELCOME TO STOCKHOLM

 one of Scandinavia's most beautiful cities, is gently spread across 14 islands. Stockholm draws visitors from all over the world with its cobblestone streets, historic architecture, and colorful fusion of contemporary and tradition. Jane, a voracious traveler with a hunger for new adventures, set off for this alluring city, eager to immerse herself in its rich culture and illustrious past.

The Stockholm archipelago emerged as Jane's plane plummeted through an orange-and-pink-hued sky, with each island having its own distinct personality and allure. As she considered the experiences that awaited her in this Scandinavian utopia, her excitement rose.

Jane was welcomed by the crisp Nordic air as soon as she stepped off the plane, which carried echoes of legends from years ago. She set out to explore the city's center with her bags in tow. She was immediately mesmerized by the streets of Gamla Stan, Stockholm's historic district. She was guided through a labyrinth of warm ochre-colored medieval buildings along cobblestone pathways. She was enticed to partake in a typical Swedish fika, which is a moment of reflection followed by a hot beverage and a sweet treat, by the aroma of freshly cooked cinnamon buns wafting from small cafes.

Jane was navigating the city when she saw how seamlessly old and new coexisted. The Royal Palace served as a monument to Sweden's regal past with its splendor and graceful facades. The nearby ABBA Museum honored the nation's contributions to modern culture while letting visitors sing and dance to well-known songs.

Jane resumed her journey to Djurgrden, an island haven that provided a break from the bustle of the city. While the Vasa Museum held her in amazement with its stunningly restored 17th-century battleship that loomed within its confines, the lush Djurgrden Park tempted her for a leisurely stroll. The ship served as a tragic reminder of the transience of human achievements after once being a magnificent work of art.

One evening, Jane made the decision to take a boat excursion to see Stockholm's distinctive archipelago splendor. As she navigated between the islands, she took in the exquisite bridges that joined them as the sun shed a golden glow across the sea. Her heart was forever changed as she saw the city's lit skyline against a backdrop of a Nordic sunset.

Jane's tour of Stockholm included its gastronomic culture as well. She enjoyed Swedish specialties like gravlax and meatballs, each one a tribute to the nation's rich culinary history. When she ventured beyond the conventional, she came into a developing food culture that merged international influences with regional ingredients to produce gastronomic marvels that piqued her interest.

Jane's visit was, however, most likely remembered for the warmth and kindness of the locals. Jane discovered that the residents of Stockholm emanated a genuine feeling of warmth that made her feel like more than simply a visitor. This was true whether she was conversing with shops, swapping travel tales with other tourists, or asking for directions from a stranger.

Jane thought back on the wide range of experiences she had gained as her stay in Stockholm came to an end. Stockholm had wrapped its enchantment around her as she strolled through its historic streets and savored the local cuisine. With a heart overflowing with appreciation for the remarkable adventure she had started in the Swedish capital, Jane boarded her return flight. The city's distinctive blend of history, modernism, nature, and culture had made an immeasurable effect.

Chapter 1: Introduction

An overview of Stockholm's history

The history of Sweden's capital city, Stockholm, dates back more than 700 years. A complex fusion of cultural, political, and economic processes that have formed its identity into the thrivi

ng metropolis it is today are entwined with its fascinating past.

Due to its advantageous location along the Baltic Sea, Stockholm, which was established in the 13th century, quickly became a significant trading hub.

With its cobblestone alleys and medieval buildings, the Old Town (Gamla Stan) serves as a tangible reminder of this time period. The 17th century, sometimes known as the "Swedish Empire" era, when Sweden expanded its power throughout the Baltic region, also left its impact on the history of the city.

The Vasa shipwreck in 1628 ranks as one of Stockholm's most important historical incidents. The Vasa, a battleship built to display Sweden's naval might, sank during her first voyage. Today, this marine tragedy is displayed at the painstakingly restored Vasa Museum, giving tourists an insight into Sweden's maritime history.

Stockholm underwent industry and modernization in the 18th and 19th centuries, which caused it to grow outside of the Old Town. The city's growth intensified in the 20th century, when renowned buildings like City Hall, which is famous for hosting the Nobel Prize dinner, transformed the city's skyline.

During World War II, the city's fortitude was put to the test as Sweden stayed neutral but encountered difficulties because of its proximity to the fighting. Following the war, Stockholm flourished as a hub of innovation and culture, giving rise to illustrious organizations like the Karolinska Institute and serving as the venue for the 1912 Summer Olympics.

Stockholm has earned a reputation for having a good standard of living, progressive principles, and technical breakthroughs. It has a multicultural population, many museums, and a thriving artistic scene. Stockholm's many attractions include the old Gamla Stan, the contemporary buildings of Norrmalm, the parks in Djurgrden, and the hip areas. Stockholm's history is an enthralling voyage through time, from its medieval origins to its modern vitality.

Stockholm's climate

Stockholm has a mild marine climate with distinct seasons that influence its weather patterns all year round. The Baltic Sea and the nearby water bodies have a significant impact on the city's climate.

Stockholm experiences chilly,

snowy winters with frequently subfreezing temperatures. It frequently snows, turning the city into a winter paradise. The Stockholm area's archipelago occasionally freezes over, making ice skating and ice fishing possible.

As the temperatures gradually rise and nature emerges from its winter hibernation, spring ushers in a gradual thaw. The summers here are generally temperate and pleasant, with average highs and lows of 60 to 70 degrees Fahrenheit (18 to 24 degrees Celsius). During this summer, the city has more daylight hours, which creates a fun atmosphere for outdoor events like festivals and picnics as well as boat trips along the rivers.

The city's parks and woodlands change color as autumn ushers in a transition to cooler temperatures and spectacular foliage. The amount of rainfall is rather evenly distributed throughout the year, with late summer and early autumn seeing a little increase.

The climate of Stockholm contributes to its allure and diversity by allowing locals and visitors to take advantage of a variety of weather patterns and seasonal activities. The city's climate significantly influences its cultural and recreational offers, whether it's ice skating on frozen waterways in the winter or taking advantage of the long summer days.

Time to visit is best

A lot depends on your preferences and the kind of experience you're looking for when deciding when to visit Stockholm. The Swedish capital's four distinct seasons each have their own charm and activities to offer.

The summer (June to August) is undoubtedly the busiest season to travel to Stockholm. Outdoor activities, festivals, and a thriving café culture bring the city to life. Average temperatures range from 18 to 24°C (64 to 75°F), which is warm and pleasant. The days are long, and you may take advantage of the famous midnight sun, allowing you plenty of time to tour the archipelago, visit sites, and engage in a variety of water sports.

Spring (April to May): The city really comes to life in the spring after the winter. Parks and gardens bloom as the temperature rises and the days lengthen, resulting in a gorgeous setting. Compared to the summer, it is a more tranquil time, making it perfect for seeing historical buildings, museums, and attractive neighborhoods without the crowds.

Autumn (September to October): The city transforms into a colorful canvas as the leaves change color throughout the fall. There is more peace and quiet because the weather is still nice and fewer tourists are around. It's the ideal season to take leisurely strolls around the parks, take in cultural events, and savor the regional fare.

Winter (December to February): Stockholm can be enchanted in the winter for people who appreciate winter activities and the warm atmosphere of the holiday season. Even though it can go below zero, the city's Christmas markets, ice rinks, and cultural activities provide a distinctive experience. In Sweden's northern regions, you might even be fortunate enough to see the Northern Lights.

The best time to travel to Stockholm ultimately depends on your interests. Plan your trip between June and August if you're drawn to outdoor activities, long daylight hours, and the lively mood of summer. Visit around spring or fall if you want to experience the changing seasons and prefer fewer crowds. And if you're looking forward to wintertime events and holiday celebrations, December to February can be your top choice.

Getting there

Stockholm's well-connected transit system makes getting there easy and convenient. There are several ways to get to the Swedish capital, whether you're coming from inside Europe or elsewhere in the world.

By Air: Arlanda Airport (ARN) and Bromma Airport (BMA) are Stockholm's two primary airports. The main and most busy airport is Arlanda, which is roughly 40 kilometers north of the city center. It provides a variety of flights from worldwide hub cities. The closer-to-the-city Bromma Airport mostly serves local and a few international destinations.

By Train: Sweden offers a reliable and comfortable rail network, making this a viable alternative for travel. Through the resund Bridge, Stockholm Centralstation, sometimes known as Stockholm C, has excellent connections to major Swedish cities as well as other nations like Norway and Denmark.

By Bus: Long-distance buses are another affordable option for getting to Stockholm. Bus routes are run by a number of firms from several European cities, providing a more economical option than flying or using the train.

By Car: Road travels can be a beautiful way to get to Stockholm if you're traveling from a nearby country or enjoy the flexibility of driving. Major highways and roads connect the city well, and driving through the Swedish countryside can be beautiful.

By Ferry: Given that Stockholm is an archipelago, ferries can be a fun method to travel there. With neighboring Baltic Sea nations like Finland, Estonia, and Latvia, ferry routes connect

Stockholm. The fact that these ships frequently include cabins adds to the experience.

Once in Stockholm, it is simple to get around and see the many areas and attractions thanks to the effective public transit system in the city, which includes buses, trams, and the metro. With numerous dedicated bike lanes and bike-sharing programs, biking is also a well-liked and environmentally friendly option.

15 reasons to book a vacation

- Historical Charm: Immerse yourself in centuries of history as you stroll through Gamla Stan, Stockholm's Old Town, and its beautiful medieval alleyways.

- Beautiful Archipelago: Explore the singular beauty of Stockholm's archipelago, which offers breathtaking boat tours and island hopping.

- Enjoy the thriving arts scene and world-class museums in the city, including the Moderna Museum and the Vasa Museum.

- Nordic Cuisine: Savor the flavors of Swedish food, from classics like meatballs to avant-garde culinary experiences at Michelin-starred establishments.

- Outdoor Adventures: Take advantage of the city's numerous parks, forests, and waterways to engage in outdoor pursuits like kayaking, cycling, and hiking.

- Experience the mesmerizing midnight sun phenomena in the summer when the lengthy daytime hours are ideal for exploring.

- Visit Stockholm's regal residences, including the Royal Palace and Drottningholm Palace, which are both rich in regal tradition.

- Innovative Design: Visit locations like the Swedish Centre for Architecture and Design to learn more about the city's reputation for outstanding design.

- Festivals aplenty: Participate in the city's energetic festivals, which highlight its open character. Examples include the Midsummer celebrations and Stockholm Pride.

- Enjoy the cosy atmosphere of Stockholm in the winter, with its Christmas markets, ice skating, and potential for seeing the Northern Lights.

- Experience Stockholm's dedication to sustainability, from its parks to its eco-friendly modes of transportation.

- Discover the distinctive characteristics of numerous areas, each of which offers a special fusion of culture, shopping, and dining.

- Take part in the local tradition of using saunas to relax and unwind, or perhaps take a cool plunge in the Baltic Sea.

- Modern Landmarks: Take in the city's cutting-edge side by admiring modern architectural wonders like the Ericsson Globe and Stockholm Waterfront.

- Benefit from the city's efficient public transit system, which makes it simple to explore every nook and cranny.

Your next holiday should be spent in Stockholm.

- Choose Stockholm as the location of your next holiday and get ready to go on a journey rich in fascinating history, breathtaking natural beauty, and exciting cultural activities. Every traveler can find something to enjoy in this Scandinavian jewel.

- Historical Charm: Gamla Stan, Stockholm's ancient Old Town, is home to cobblestone streets where centuries of history come to life. Admire beautifully maintained structures while immersing yourself in historical tales.

- Adventure in the Archipelago: Explore the fascinating appeal of Stockholm's vast archipelago. Take boat excursions to discover lovely towns, breathtaking vistas, and calm waters.

- Engage in Stockholm's thriving cultural sector, which is home to internationally renowned museums, galleries, and theaters. You'll be enthralled by artistic expressions everywhere you go, from the famous Vasa Museum to modern art venues.

- Scenic Beauty: During the summer, when the city enjoys longer daylight hours, bask in the majesty of the midnight sun. Enjoy Stockholm's natural beauty, which is defined by its lush parks, tranquil woodlands, and glistening rivers.

- Enjoy the culinary delights of Nordic cuisine, from traditional Swedish meatballs to cutting-edge dining experiences. Enjoy tastes that showcase the culinary quality and cultural variety of the city.

- Visit the royal palaces in Stockholm to experience true royal elegance. Explore the lavish Royal Palace before taking a boat to the magnificent 17th-century Drottningholm Palace, which is inscribed on the UNESCO World Heritage List.

- Investigate the reputation of Stockholm for innovative design. Visit the Swedish Center for Architecture and Design to see how the city's contemporary style melds with its historic surroundings.

- Time your visit to coincide with one of Stockholm's vivacious festivals, which celebrate everything from music and the arts to cultural diversity and LGBTQ+ pride. Festivals and Events.

- Eco-Friendly Lifestyle: Embrace Stockholm's dedication to sustainability, from its use of sustainable transportation to its abundance of parks and other open areas. Become a part of a city that appreciates environmental awareness.

- Wander through varied neighborhoods that each have their own personality and provide a variety of places to eat, shop, and have fun.

- Stockholm offers a memorable trip because to its harmonious fusion of history, culture, and natural beauties. Stockholm welcomes you with open arms, whether you're an art aficionado, a history nerd, a nature lover, or just looking for a special vacation.

Chapter 2: Tips and considering

Budget-friendly Stockholm travel

For tourists looking to discover this dynamic city without breaking the bank, traveling to Stockholm on a tight budget may be an interesting and rewarding experience. The Swedish capital is a budget-friendly destination that combines cultural marvels, historic allure, and natural beauty.

First off, there are several inexpensive lodging options in Stockholm. Affordable lodging options include guesthouses, hostels, and low-cost hotels. To save money and still have quick access to public transit, choose lodging that is just outside the city center.

In Stockholm, public transportation is a valuable ally for visitors on a tight budget. You can get about the city's attractions without spending a fortune on cabs because to its effective and well-connected network of buses, trams, and the metro. If you want unrestricted use of the public transportation system while you're there, think about buying a travel pass.

Many of Stockholm's numerous attractions are either free or reasonably priced. Gamla Stan, the beautiful old town, is the ideal place for a leisurely stroll. It is a lovely tangle of cobblestone streets, vibrant houses, and small shops. There are many parks and green areas in the city, such Djurgrden, where people may go for walks, picnics, and even free outdoor concerts in the summer.

Numerous museums and galleries give free admission to those who are interested in the arts and cultures on particular days or during particular hours. For free access to world-class art collections, the Moderna Museet and the Nationalmuseum are worth a visit.

Expensive culinary experiences are not always necessary. Discovering neighborhood markets like stermalms saluhall allows you to experience Swedish cuisine without paying the high restaurant prices. To experience the flavors of the city without going over budget, choose economical street cuisine or grab a quick snack at neighborhood cafés.

How to navigate Stockholm

Take the bus or train.

 The wide and effective public transit network in Stockholm is a terrific way to move around the city without breaking the bank. A single ticket costs 39 SEK (about $4 USD), and a day pass costs 165 SEK (around $15 USD). A 72-hour pass costs 330 SEK (about $30 USD) and can save you money if you're going to use public transit regularly.

Map of the Stockholm public transportation system

Benefit from free walking tours.

In Stockholm, there are several free walking tours that are a terrific opportunity to see the city and discover its history and culture. These excursions often cover many neighborhoods and run for a few hours.

Stockholm walking tours for free Opens a new window

Throughout the city on a bike.

 Cycling is a terrific method to travel around Stockholm without spending a lot of money because it is such a bike-friendly city. For around 200 SEK (around $20

USD) per day, you may rent a bike from one of the many bike shops in the city.

In Stockholm, bicycles opens a fresh window cities-today.com

In Stockholm, bicycles

By boat, tour the archipelago

Over 30,000 islands form an archipelago that surrounds Stockholm, providing a unique viewpoint of the city. A variety of various boat cruises are offered, with prices ranging from 200 SEK (about $20 USD) to 500 SEK (around $50 USD). By watercraft, the Stockholm Archipelago opens a fresh window

Stockholm's shopping

- The main shopping district of Stockholm, Drottninggatan, is home to a wide range of retailers, including H&M, Zara, and Sephora. You should budget approximately 500 SEK (or $50 USD) every hour for shopping here.
- Stockholm's Drottninggatan shopping districtOpens in a new window

  Stockholm's Drottninggatan shopping district
- Gamla Stan, Stockholm's historic district, is home to a multitude of quaint boutiques and antique stores. Here you can get uncommon presents and souvenirs, but expect to pay a premium. Gamla Stan shopping can cost up to 1000 SEK (around $100 USD) per hour.
- Stockholm's Gamla Stan shopping districtopens a fresh window

  Stockholm's Gamla Stan shopping district
- Nordiska Kompaniet is a retail establishment that was founded in 1902. It's an excellent location to find premium Swedish design goods. You should budget

approximately 1000 SEK (or $100 USD) every hour for shopping at NK.

- Stockholm's Nordiska Kompaniet department storeOpens in a new window Stockholm's Nordiska Kompaniet department store

- The Hötorget flea market is an excellent place to find used goods including furniture and clothing. From 10 a.m. until 5 p.m. on Saturdays and Sundays, it is open. At Hötorget, you may anticipate spending about 500 SEK (about $50 USD) each hour on shopping.
  Stockholm's flea market Hötorget

- Beyond Retro: There are two of these vintage clothes shops in Stockholm. Unique items from the 1950s through the 1990s are available. While prices at Beyond Retro vary, you can anticipate to pay about 500 SEK (or $50 USD) each hour there.

5 affordable hotel alternatives in Stockholm

Generator Stockholm: All of the main attrGeneratoractions are within easy walking distance of this hostel, which is situated in the center of the city. Along with a bar, a restaurant, and a game area, it features a selection of private and dorm rooms. Price per night starts at about 500 SEK ($50 USD).

Hostel Generator Stockholm, Stockholm

The Ibis Styles Stockholm Odenplan: is a hotel next to the Odenplan metro station in Stockholm's Norrmalm neighborhood. It boasts straightforward, contemporary rooms that are equipped with all the comforts of home. Price per night starts at about 700 SEK ($70 USD

.Stoc

kholm's Ibis Styles Stockholm Odenplan hotel

Rex Petit: The Mariatorget metro station is just a short stroll from this hotel, which is situated in Stockholm's Södermalm neighborhood. It boasts quaint Scandinavian-style tiny, cozily furnished rooms. The starting price for a night is roughly 600 SEK ($60 USD).

Hotel Rex Petit in Stockholmopens a fresh window

Connect Hotel City: This hotel is situated near the Central Station in Stockholm's Norrmalm neighborhood. It boasts minimalistic, contemporary rooms. Price per night starts at about 800 SEK ($80

USD).

Söder Hostel Stockholm: A short distance from the Slussen metro station, Stockholm's Söder Hostel is situated in the Södermalm neighborhood. It offers a selection of private rooms and dorm rooms in addition to a bar, a restaurant, and a roof terrace with breathtaking city views. Price per night starts at about 400 SEK ($40 USD).

5 opulent accommodations in Stockholm

Grand Hotel: Overlooking the Royal Palace, this historic hotel is situated in the center of Stockholm. There is a rooftop bar with magnificent city views, a Michelin-starred restaurant, and a sumptuous spa. The cost of a room per night starts at about 20,000

SEK ($2,000 USD).

Stockholm's Grand HotelOpens in a separate window

Hotel Diplomat: This classy hotel is situated near the Nobel Museum in Stockholm's stermalm neighborhood. It offers a sauna, a workout facility, and a lovely garden. The cost of a room per night starts at about 15,000 SEK ($1,500 USD).

Stockholm's Diplomat Hotelopens a fresh window

The Fotografiska Museum: is not far from Stockholm's Nordic Light Hotel, which is a contemporary hotel. It offers a restaurant, a bar, and a rooftop pool with breathtaking city views.

The cost of a room per night starts at about 10,000 SEK ($1,000 USD).

At Six: This chic hotel is situated near the Central Station in Stockholm's Norrmalm neighborhood.

There is a bar, a sauna, and a gym there.

The nightly rate for rooms begins at about 12,000 SEK ($1,200 USD).

Hotel Skeppsholmen: On the island of Skeppsholmen, in the center of Stockholm, is the boutique hotel known as Hotel Skeppsholmen. It features a spa, a sauna, and a rooftop patio with breathtaking city views. The cost of a room per night starts at about 14,000 SEK ($1,400 USD).

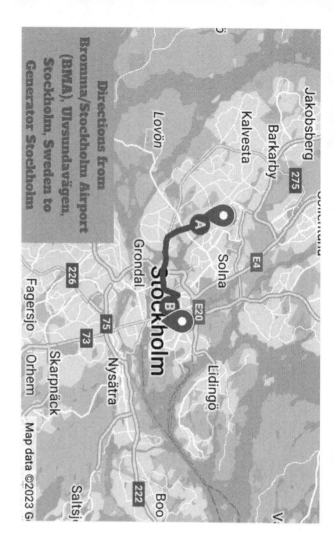

Directions from
Bromma/Stockholm Airport
(BMA), Ulvsundavägen,
Stockholm, Sweden to
Generator Stockholm

Directions from
Bromma/Stockholm Airport
(BMA), Ulvsundavägen,
Stockholm, Sweden to The Ibis
Styles Stockholm Odenplan

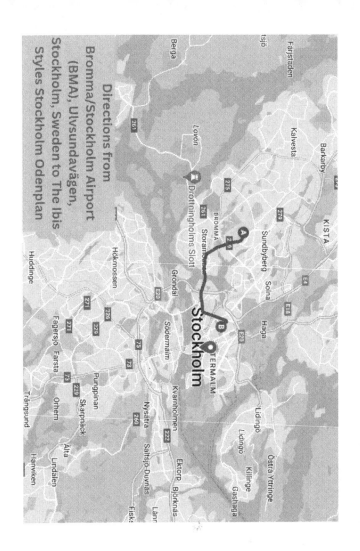

41

Directions from Bromma/Stockholm
Airport (BMA), Ulvsundavägen,
Stockholm, Sweden to Rex Petit,
Luntmakargatan, Stockholm, Sweden

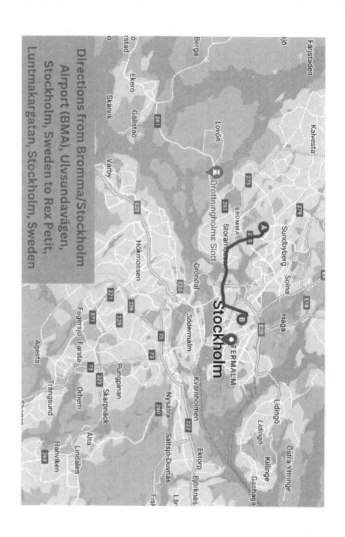

42

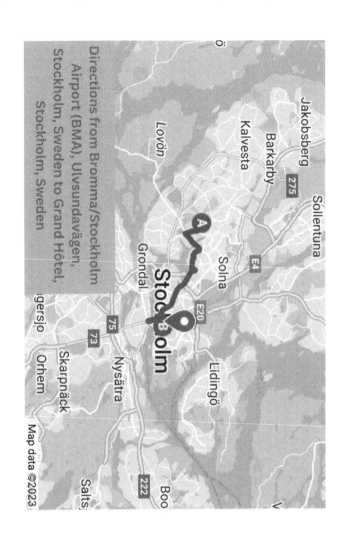

Directions from Bromma/Stockholm Airport (BMA), Ulvsundavägen, Stockholm, Sweden to Grand Hôtel, Stockholm, Sweden

43

Directions from Bromma/Stockholm Airport (BMA), Ulvsundavägen, Stockholm, Sweden to Hotel Diplomat, Strandvägen, Stockholm, Sweden

Chapter 3: Top 5 event in Stockholm to attend

The annual Stockholm Music & Arts Festival: is a real treat for music lovers. The Stockholm Music

& Arts Festival, which takes place in August, turns the lovely island of Skeppsholmen into a haven for music fans. The concert features a broad range of regional, national, and worldwide performers in the rock, pop, electronic, and independent genres. An remarkable experience is created by the distinctive fusion of live concerts, art displays, and breathtaking waterfront vistas.

Stockholm is the location of the Nobel Prize ceremony and banquet, one of the most distinguished honors in the world. Every year, on December 10, the day of Alfred Nobel's passing, the Nobel Prize Ceremony is held. Nobel laureates, members of the Swedish royal family, and eminent guests from around the world attend the event, which is hosted at the Stockholm Concert Hall. After the ceremony, a magnificent banquet is held at Stockholm City Hall where guests may see the fusion of tradition, glitz, and intelligence.

Midsummer's Eve: Midsummer is a cherished Swedish custom that is enthusiastically observed nationwide, but especially in Stockholm. Locals and guests come together to celebrate the longest day of

the year, which usually occurs in June. Some of the
highlights include dancing around the maypole,
eating traditional Swedish cuisine, and playing
games. One of the most well-known Midsummer
festivals, replete with folk music, dancing, and a
celebratory atmosphere, is held at Skansen, an
outdoor museum and zoo.

Stockholm Pride: Stockholm Pride is a vibrant and
dynamic event that takes place in July or August to
celebrate diversity and LGBTQ+ rights. A pride
parade through the center of the city, performances,
workshops, and seminars addressing various
LGBTQ+ concerns are among the events that make
up the festival's week-long schedule. Stockholm
Pride is a must-attend event for both locals and
visitors since it not only provides a platform for
advocacy but also fosters a spirit of harmony,
acceptance, and joy.

Stockholm International Film Festival: The
Stockholm International Film Festival is a
compelling event for movie lovers. This event,
which takes place every November, features an
amazing collection of foreign films, including

acclaimed art-house productions, ground-breaking documentaries, and exciting blockbusters. The festival offers a singular chance to investigate various cinematic viewpoints and converse with directors during Q&A sessions. The Stockholm International Film Festival is a cultural high point for individuals who are passionate about the big screen, with a focus on innovation and creativity.

Top 5 Stockholm attraction

Gamla Stan (Old Town): is like traveling back in time. The center of Stockholm lies this attractive medieval district, which is renowned for its winding cobblestone alleyways, vibrant structures, and ancient architecture. One of the main attractions is the Royal Palace, a spectacular baroque building. Wander around the narrow streets, look around the cute shops and art galleries, and enjoy a fika (Swedish coffee break) in lovely cafes. Stortorget, the city's central square, is a must-see because the Christmas market there makes it more charming during the winter.

Vasa Museum: a 17th-century warship that sank on its maiden voyage and was miraculously preserved in the chilly waters of Stockholm's harbor, is housed in the Vasa Museum. It is an incredible maritime treasure. This museum presents a singular chance to behold a magnificently restored ship that is adorned with complex carvings and sculptures. The exhibitions shed light on the historical setting in which the ship was built as well as the actions made to save and restore it. It is a convincing illustration of Sweden's seafaring heritage.

Skansen: The world's oldest outdoor museum, Skansen, takes tourists on a tour of Swedish history. Traditional Swedish rural architecture, including farmhouses, windmills, and workshops, is displayed in this living history museum. Skansen is unique since it's not simply a static exhibit; it's staffed with costumed workers who perform traditional music, dance, and crafts. Skansen also has a small zoo where you can get up close and personal with native Scandinavian wildlife.

Djurgrden: is a recreational island that offers a blend of cultural attractions and scenic beauty. It is a green haven in the middle of Stockholm. It is home to a number of must-see attractions, such as the Gröna Lund amusement park, the Nordic Museum, and the ABBA Museum. Picnics, leisurely walks, and bike rides can all be enjoyed on the island's lush sceneries. The waterfront promenades provide breathtaking views of the city and the neighboring archipelago during the warmer months.

City Hall and Nobel Museum: Stockholm's City Hall is a significant landmark and the site of the annual Nobel Prize banquet. It also houses the Nobel Museum. You may take guided tours to see the opulent Blue Hall, which holds the Nobel feast, and the sumptuous Golden Hall, which is decorated with mosaics. In the Nobel Museum, which is close to City Hall, you may learn about the background and accomplishments of Nobel laureates from numerous fields and gain understanding of the significance of the Nobel Prize.

3 days Stockholm itinerary

Day 1: Visit Stockholm's Gamla Stan first thing in the morning. This lovely neighborhood is full of winding cobblestone lanes, vibrant buildings, and historical sites. The Royal Palace, one of Europe's biggest palaces, is a must-see. Take a stroll down the shoreline afterward to take in the breathtaking sights of the city.

Try some typical Swedish food at a nearby restaurant for lunch. You can eat things like gravlax, herring, and meatballs. Visit the Vasa Museum in the afternoon to see the world's only nearly completely undamaged 17th-century ship. Seeing this well-preserved relic of nautical history is an amazing experience.

Day 2: Start the day by visiting the island of Djurgrden, which is renowned for its lovely gardens and museums. Visit the ABBA Museum to find out more about the renowned Swedish pop group and even to sing along to some of their hit songs. Next, proceed to Skansen, the oldest open-air museum in the world, where you can view typical Swedish homes and discover the nation's rural past.

Take a boat trip of the Stockholm archipelago in the afternoon. A opportunity to unwind and take in the amazing views are provided by this magnificent group of islands. Explore Södermalm, a hip neighborhood in Stockholm known for its antique shops, hipster cafes, and exciting nightlife, to round off your day.

Day 3: Begin the day by touring Stockholm City Hall, a majestic structure famous for serving as the site of the Nobel Prize dinner. Take a tour to discover its past and take in the magnificent architecture. After that, wander around the hipster neighborhood of stermalm, famous for its expensive shops and specialty food stores.

Visit the Fotografiska Museum in the afternoon to see examples of modern photography from throughout the globe. You can really get lost in the

art and culture there. Visit the famous Stockholm
Cathedral, a stunning illustration of Swedish brick
Gothic architecture, to cap off your journey.

7 days Stockholm itinerary

Day 1: Spend the first day of your journey touring
Stockholm's ancient Gamla Stan. Visit the Royal
Palace, meander through its winding cobblestone
lanes, and take in the quaint cafes and boutiques.
The Nobel Museum and the Storkyrkan Cathedral
should not be missed.

Day 2: Take a boat cruise to discover Stockholm's
archipelago. This is a distinctive experience with
over 30,000 islands. You may travel to some of the
bigger islands, such as Vaxholm or Sandhamn,
where you can take in the scenery, go swimming, or
just unwind.

Day 3: Travel to the island of Djurgrden, which is renowned for its parks and cultural attractions. Discover the lovely Djurgrden Park, which has a number of museums, including the ABBA Museum and the Vasa Museum, which is home to a warship from the 17th century.

Day 4: Visit the Södermalm neighborhood to get a glimpse of Stockholm's contemporary side. This trendy area is teeming with cool cafes, antique stores, and art galleries. Walk along the waterfront promenade to take in the breathtaking cityscape.

Day 5: Take a tour of the Skansen Open-Air Museum, the oldest outdoor museum in existence. You may discover Swedish history, culture, and customs here. Do not pass up the opportunity to view the Nordic creatures in the zoo area.

Day 6: Visit the Fotografiska Museum on day six to view works by Swedish and international photographers. There is always something new and

intriguing to see because the exhibitions are
frequently changed.

Day 7: Pay a visit to Stockholm City Hall to cap off
your vacation. Take a tour with a guide to see the
stunning building and out more about the banquet
for the Nobel Prize that is held here each year. For
sweeping views of the city, don't forget to climb the
tower.

Just keep in mind that this is only a suggestion; you
may always modify it to suit your needs and tastes.
Stockholm offers a lot, from its beautiful
architecture to its thriving cultural scene.

Chatper 4: planning a trip to Stockholm

A vacation to Stockholm provides a fascinating fusion of tradition, culture, and modernity. The capital of Sweden is a city of islands, bridges, and lively neighborhoods, making it the perfect place for tourists looking for a distinctive European experience.

The first step in any trip is investigation. Choose the ideal time to visit as a first step. With longer days and great weather for exploring, summer, which lasts from June to August, is the busiest travel season. Consider going, though, if you're hoping for a less expensive and crowded experience, in the shoulder seasons of spring (April-May) or fall (September-October).

Stockholm offers a wide variety of lodging alternatives, from opulent hotels to inviting boutique motels. Gamla Stan (the Old Town), Norrmalm, and Södermalm are excellent alternatives for central locations since they provide quick access to attractions and public transportation.

Speaking of transportation, Stockholm has an effective and well-connected public transportation system. It is affordable to move around thanks to the Stockholm Card's unrestricted entry to buses, trams, ferries, and several museums.

The city offers a wide variety of must-see attractions for tourists. Explore Gamla Stan's lovely cobblestone streets, which are filled with historic structures, adorable boutiques, and the Royal Palace. Don't miss the ABBA Museum for a glimpse of legendary Swedish pop culture or the Vasa Museum, which displays a flawlessly preserved warship from the 17th century.

The gourmet scene in Stockholm will excite foodies. Try classic Swedish fare like meatballs, herring, and gravlax or treat yourself to Michelin-starred restaurants' innovative Nordic cuisine.

Explore Stockholm's surrounding archipelago, which includes some 30,000 islands and islets, by venturing outside of the city core. Ferries and boats provide access to hiking trails, island hopping, and the tranquil natural beauty of the area.

What to pack for your trip

- **Layers of Clothing:** Even in the summer, Stockholm's weather may be erratic. Bring a variety of thin layers, such as t-shirts, long sleeve shirts, sweaters, and a functional jacket. In this manner, you can quickly adapt to the fluctuating daytime temperatures.
-
- You'll be walking a lot while visiting Stockholm's parks, streets, and sights, so wear comfortable shoes. It is essential to use supportive walking shoes. Packing a pair of fashionable, yet sturdy shoes that can handle the city's cobblestone streets is a good idea.

- Stockholm is renowned for its sporadic showers of rain, even in the summer. To stay dry and cozy, pack a small, waterproof jacket or umbrella.

- Be sure to have the appropriate power adapters for your electronic equipment.

Type C and Type F power outlets are used in Sweden, therefore bring the necessary adapters.

- **Electronics:** Keep in mind to pack your camera, smartphone, and any other gadgets you intend to use while traveling. For keeping your devices charged while you're on the go, a power bank can be useful.

- **trip documents:** You must have your passport, a visa, details of your trip insurance, and any tickets or reservations you may need. Make electronic copies of these documents, and keep them in a safe online location.

- **Reusable Water Bottle:** The tap water in Stockholm is excellent and safe to drink. You may save plastic trash while staying hydrated by bringing a reusable water bottle.

- **Sun protection:** The sun can be very powerful throughout the summer. Bring sunblock, sunglasses, and a cap with you as UV protection.

- Put your toiletries, together with any prescription drugs, in a travel-sized toiletry bag. Remember that many hotels offer basic toiletries, so before overpacking in this category, verify with your lodging.

- Having a printed map or travel guide can be quite helpful for touring the city without relying exclusively on digital gadgets, even though smartphones have made navigation simpler.

- Consider bringing swimwear if you're visiting in the summer. Saunas and spa services are accessible at many hotels in Stockholm, and you might even like to swim in the waters of the adjacent archipelago.

Stockholm's nightlife

The nightlife in Stockholm is a thriving, varied scene that appeals to a wide range of tastes and inclinations. The Swedish capital comes alive after sunset, offering something for everyone, from hip bars and nightclubs to live music venues and cultural activities.

The area of Södermalm is one of the most well-known hotspots for the city's nightlife. The bohemian vibe, busy streets, and diverse selection of bars and clubs in this region are well-known. You can find everything from hipster bars to jazz lounges on the streets of Södermalm, each with an own atmosphere.

Stockholm offers a flourishing music scene for individuals who like live music. Concerts featuring anything from indie rock and pop to jazz and electronic music are held in places like Debaser, Nalen, and Fasching. These venues offer a wide range of musical possibilities by showcasing both regional musicians and artists from around the world.

In Stockholm, nightclubs are a big magnet for people who want to dance the night away. Numerous posh nightclubs can be found in the Stureplan neighborhood, which is frequently referred to be the city's party hub. These establishments draw both locals and tourists. These clubs provide an exceptional nightlife experience with top-notch DJs, stunning light displays, and a chic ambiance.

Stockholm features theaters and performance venues where you can catch a range of performances, including ballet, opera, and theatrical productions, if you're looking for a more cultural evening. Among the notable locations where these artistic performances are presented are the Royal Swedish Opera and the Stockholm City Theatre.

In terms of drinking, Stockholm has embraced the idea of "afterwork," when professionals congregate at bars for socializing after work hours. Due to this, there is a burgeoning pub culture with a focus on specialty cocktails, beers brewed locally, and quaint lounges.

The nightlife in Stockholm can be a bit pricy, but the quality of the experiences is frequently well worth it, it's crucial to remember that. As the evening wears on, the nightlife scene also tends to pick up, with many locations getting busier around 10 PM.

People and Culture

The inhabitants of Stockholm and its culture represent a harmonious fusion of tradition, modernity, and a strong respect for the arts. The cordial nature, openness, and respect for personal space of the Swedes provide for an inviting environment for visitors to fully immerse themselves in the culture.

The Swedish idea of "lagom," which translates to "just the right amount," permeates daily life in Stockholm and is a key part of Swedish culture. This school of thought places a significant emphasis on equality, balance, and moderation. Stockholm is a place where people from different backgrounds can feel at home because Swedes respect inclusivity and work to establish a society where everyone's needs are addressed.

The city's culture thrives thanks to its long history and contemporary development. With well-preserved medieval structures set opposite sleek, modern structures, Stockholm's architecture is a reflection of its past. Gamla Stan (Old Town) boasts small cobblestone alleyways that give off a medieval beauty, while Norrmalm showcases contemporary skyscrapers and creative urban design.

Design and art are essential to the character of Stockholm. Numerous galleries, museums, and design studios in the city showcase both time-honored craftsmanship and cutting-edge ingenuity. The Fotografiska museum is devoted to international photography, while the Moderna Museet exhibits modern and contemporary art. Visitors can learn about regional design ideas in the city's shops and exhibitions. Swedish design giants like IKEA and H&M have made a lasting impression on world culture.

Stockholm's culinary scene combines traditional Swedish cuisine with global influences. Food lovers can enjoy a wide variety of gastronomic delights, from the legendary smörgsbord to cutting-edge Nordic cuisine. The city's devotion to environmental awareness is reflected in restaurants' frequent emphasis on locally produced ingredients and sustainable procedures.

The Stockholm calendar is punctuated by festivals and celebrations that provide a window into contemporary festivities and Swedish customs. A few examples of the city's vibrant cultural calendar are Lucia Day, a festival of light during the gloomy winter months, and Midsummer's Eve, which marks the summer solstice.

Chapter 5: The top 10 local dishes to sample in Stockholm

Meatballs from Sweden (Köttbullar): These delicious meatballs, which are a traditional Swedish dish, are normally made from a mixture of ground meat, frequently a combination of beef and pig, and are typically served with lingonberry sauce and creamy mashed potatoes.

Gravel salmon or gravlax: that has been finely sliced and marinated in dill, sugar, and salt is the main ingredient in the gravad lax meal. It's a delicate dish that perfectly conveys the sea's freshness.

Sill or herring: is a common ingredient in Swedish cooking and can be served fried, pickled, or smoked. It is frequently offered with a variety of sides as part of a buffet.

bread Skagen: A posh open-faced sandwich that is made by layering a shrimp salad dressing over buttered bread. The blending of flavors and textures delights the palate.

Rrakor: These delicious, crispy potato pancakes are served with sour cream, caviar, or smoked salmon as a comfort food.

(rtsoppa med Pannkakor) Pea Soup with Pancakes: This substantial yellow pea soup, a traditional Thursday dish, is frequently eaten with thin pancakes and lingonberries.

Janssons Frestelse: also known as "Jansson's Temptation," is a creamy potato and anchovy casserole that is a comfort food classic and frequently served at Christmas.

Kanelbulle: Savor the aroma of kanelbullar, or freshly made cinnamon buns. These delicious sweets go well with a cup of coffee.

Pie prepared with the distinctive and tasty Västerbotten cheese: Västerbotten Cheese Pie offers the ideal balance of creaminess and sharpness.

Lingonberry Jam: Although not a complete meal in and of itself, lingonberry jam is a common side that goes well with many Swedish cuisine. Various meats and desserts go well with its tangy-sweet flavor.

Spend wisely and travel safely

Travelers who set out for the intriguing city of
Stockholm will find a seamless fusion of old-world
beauty and contemporary innovation there. It's
critical to balance your spending and put safety first
if you want to get the most out of your vacation.

Make a budget for your trip before you leave.
Stockholm is renowned for its premium retail areas
and fine, but frequently expensive, dining
alternatives. There are, nevertheless, many cost-

effective methods to take use of the city. Choose regional street cuisine or browse the nearby markets for fresh goods and reasonably priced snacks. Think about getting a Stockholm Pass, which provides access to numerous attractions and public transportation, allowing you to make the most of your trip while saving money.

You should prioritize safety when making your trip arrangements. Despite Stockholm's well-deserved reputation as one of the safest cities in the world, it's always a good idea to exercise caution. Keep your possessions safe, especially when using public transportation or in crowded settings. Learn the local customs and emergency contact information so you can navigate any unforeseen situations.

Remember to go beyond the well-known tourist attractions as you explore all that Stockholm has to offer. Explore the Gamla Stan (Old Town), which features quaint cobblestone streets and colorful houses, but also go for the less well-known areas to get a sense of the true local culture. Utilize the city's effective public transit system to go to different parts of the city, which includes buses, trams, and the metro.

Take time into account to get the most out of your trip. Pack for a range of weather because Stockholm's weather can be fickle. The busiest travel season is summer, when more outdoor events and longer daylight hours are available. However, traveling in the off-peak months of spring and fall may offer excellent weather and fewer visitors.

Local customs and etiquette

Stockholm, the capital of Sweden, is a city rich in history and culture, and its local customs and etiquette reflect this unique blend. When visiting Stockholm, it's essential to understand and respect the customs that define the social fabric of the city.

One prominent aspect of local etiquette in Stockholm is the concept of "lagom," which translates to "just the right amount" or "moderation." Swedes value balance and avoid extremes in their behavior, conversations, and even consumption. It's considered polite to be reserved and not overly expressive, both in public spaces and private gatherings. This cultural norm is evident in their subtle gestures, calm demeanor, and an emphasis on equality in social interactions.

The practice of "fika" is another key cultural trait. Fika is more than just a coffee break – it's a cherished tradition of pausing for a moment to enjoy coffee or tea accompanied by pastries or light snacks. This communal pause provides an opportunity for meaningful conversations, fostering relationships and connections.

Swedish punctuality is an integral part of etiquette. Arriving on time for appointments, meetings, and social gatherings is highly valued. It demonstrates respect for others' time and commitment to maintaining a smoothly functioning society.

When it comes to dining etiquette, many restaurants in Stockholm embrace the concept of "smorgasbord," offering a variety of dishes. Politeness dictates that you should take moderate portions at first to ensure everyone can enjoy the spread. Additionally, it's customary to finish everything on your plate, as wasting food is generally frowned upon.

When interacting with locals, a firm handshake, direct eye contact, and addressing people by their last name and title (Mr. or Ms.) until invited otherwise are common practices. Small talk often revolves around neutral subjects like the weather or cultural events before delving into more personal matters.

In terms of dress code, Stockholm's style is typically casual but polished. People take pride in their appearance and dressing appropriately for different occasions is seen as a sign of respect.

Understanding and embracing these local customs and etiquettes while in Stockholm not only ensures a smoother interaction with the locals but also allows you to immerse yourself in the city's rich cultural tapestry.

travel within Stockholm

Traveling through Stockholm gives a fascinating
tour of a place where old-world beauty and cutting-
edge elegance coexist harmoniously. The gorgeous
waterfronts, verdant parks, and fine architecture of
the Swedish capital, which is stretched across 14
islands, are a visual delight. You'll discover that this
thriving metropolitan center's attractions cater to a
wide variety of interests as you explore it.

Start your tour by exploring Gamla Stan, the
fascinating historic town from the Middle Ages.
Grand palaces like the Royal Palace and Stockholm
Cathedral are reached by cobblestone streets that
weave past colorful houses. Spend some time
getting lost in the tiny lanes lined with shops, cafes,
and art galleries showcasing both traditional and
modern Swedish culture.

The Vasa Museum is a must-see if you want to see
Stockholm's vast cultural diversity. It allows you to
travel back in time and admire the precise
craftsmanship of a bygone era because it is home to

the flawlessly preserved Vasa, a battleship from the 17th century. The nearby ABBA Museum immerses visitors in the world of the renowned musical group by providing hands-on exhibitions and the opportunity to dance to their immortal tunes.

Djurgrden, a green island home to several attractions including Skansen, the oldest open-air museum in the world, is a haven for nature lovers. Here, historical structures from various eras dot the landscape, taking you back in time to Sweden. In addition, Gröna Lund, an amusement park with thrilling rides and a lively atmosphere, is included in the lush expanse of Djurgrden.

Experience the Midnight Sun phenomena in the summer or the Northern Lights in the winter as twilight envelops the city. The dining scene in Stockholm is equally alluring, with traditional Swedish food coexisting peacefully with other influences. Visit neighborhood cafés and seaside restaurants to indulge in Swedish meatballs, scrumptious herring dishes, and delicious pastries.

The experience of traveling in Stockholm is a symphony of old-world charm and contemporary wonders, whether you're wandering through Södermalm's trendy districts, enjoying a boat tour through the archipelago, or unwinding in a traditional Swedish sauna. The city is one of Europe's most alluring places, as evidenced by its capacity to enthrall visitors with its rich history, cultural treasures, and stunning environment.

Chapter 6: Advice and Thoughts

regard for Social Norms: The civility and regard for private space that the Swedes are known for. Keep a reasonable distance from other people and avoid having loud talks when in public settings. Positive encounters are often aided by being respectful and polite.

The majority of Stockholm is a cashless society. The use of credit and debit cards is common, even for modest purchases. To prevent any payment issues, make sure to have a card on hand and think about telling your bank about your vacation plans.

Sustainable Transportation: Stockholm's transportation alternatives reflect the city's dedication to sustainability. Use the effective public transit network, which consists of the T-bana, trams, and buses. Instead, embrace cycling; the city is bike-friendly and provides rental options for simple exploring.

Smoking Restrictions: Smoking is not permitted in a lot of public places, such as eateries, coffee shops, and interior spaces. Always abide by specified smoking areas to avoid penalties and show consideration for others' comfort.

Purchases of alcohol: Systembolaget, the government-owned stores, are the only places where alcoholic beverages are sold. Remember that these shops have limited hours, particularly on weekends and holidays. If you intend to buy alcohol while traveling, make plans in advance.

Tipping customs: Compared to some other nations, Sweden does not tip as frequently. Although service fees are sometimes included in restaurant bills, it is nevertheless nice to round up the total or leave a little tip for really good service. Small tips are often appreciated by cab drivers.

Language: Even though many Swedes are fluent in English, it's polite to learn a few fundamental Swedish expressions. A simple "Hej" or "Tack" might go a long way in demonstrating your respect for the native way of life.

Cultural Sites: Be mindful of any regulations governing photographing, touching artifacts, and keeping a respectful approach when touring museums or other cultural institutions. All visitors will have a positive experience thanks to this, which will also aid in maintaining the integrity of the antiques.

entry prerequisites

Visa and passport requirements: The majority of visitors to Stockholm, including those from the United States, Canada, and many European nations, are exempt from visa requirements for short stays (usually up to 90 days) engaged in tourism, business, or family visits. However, it's imperative to make sure your passport is still valid at least six months after the date you plan to depart. Make sure to submit your application through the Swedish embassy or consulate well in advance if you are a national of a nation that needs a Schengen visa.

Travel Restrictions for COVID-19: Entry criteria are subject to change due to the continuing worldwide epidemic. Before you fly, make sure to check the most recent information from the Swedish government and the applicable airline. As of my most recent update, depending on your level of immunization and the current COVID-19 scenario, testing and quarantine requirements might be necessary.

Customs Declaration: Pay close attention to Swedish customs laws. To prevent penalties or confiscation, declare any commodities, such as alcohol, tobacco, and other things, that exceed the permitted limits.

Travel Insurance: Having comprehensive travel insurance is strongly advised, even though it is not a formal entrance requirement. This insurance should cover unexpected events during your stay, trip cancellations, and medical emergencies.

Immigration officials may want documentation showing where you will be residing when visiting Stockholm. A hotel reservation, a letter of invitation from a friend or relative, or other appropriate documentation can serve as proof of this.

Return Ticket: Having a return or onward ticket is recommended as proof that you intend to depart Sweden within the allotted term.

Health Warnings: Be aware of any health warnings or vaccines that may be advised or required for admission into Sweden. No specific immunizations were needed for entrance as of my most recent update, but health conditions can change.

Travel protection

Consider travel insurance before setting out on an expedition to Stockholm, one of Scandinavia's most beautiful and bustling towns, to ensure a worry-free trip. vacation insurance offers peace of mind as you explore the city's attractive streets, historic sites, and breathtaking waterfront vistas. It serves as a vital safety net against unforeseen circumstances that could interfere with or ruin your vacation plans.

Stockholm is a popular destination for tourists from all over the world because of its extensive history and contemporary cosmopolitan ambiance. Even the most precisely planned vacations, however, may run into unforeseen difficulties, such as flight cancellations, misplaced luggage, medical problems, or unanticipated travel delays. Travel insurance can help in this situation.

For vacations to Stockholm, travel insurance policies frequently offer coverage for a variety of emergencies. If you have medical coverage, you may be sure that you'll have access to high-quality care if you get sick while traveling. This is crucial in a place where the expense of healthcare for visitors can be expensive. In addition, if your vacation is canceled due to unforeseen circumstances, travel insurance might pay for non-refundable charges.

With its chilly winters and wet summers, Stockholm's weather can be erratic, raising the possibility of flight cancellations and delays. Travel insurance that covers such eventualities might offer monetary security, enabling you to rebook flights and pay for additional lodging costs.

Furthermore, Stockholm's complex archipelago and myriad waterways can provide thrilling adventures but can present dangers, especially if you're considering kayaking or boating. You can be protected in the event of accidents or injuries by purchasing travel insurance that includes coverage for adventure sports and activities.

Security and readiness

In the quickly changing world of today, ensuring the safety and readiness of a city like Stockholm is essential. The safety and security of its citizens and visitors must be given first priority in Stockholm, the capital of Sweden, which is renowned for its stunning surroundings, rich cultural history, and thriving economy. Together, the city's government and residents must reduce potential dangers and be well-equipped for any unanticipated emergency.

Preparedness for disasters is one of the most important aspects of safety in Stockholm. Due to its location near water bodies, the city may be vulnerable to specific natural calamities such heavy winter storms or flooding. So it is crucial to have detailed plans for disaster management, public awareness campaigns, and regular drills. Residents can be informed about the right steps to take during emergencies, such as evacuation procedures or communication protocols, by integrating the community in preparedness efforts.

Furthermore, Stockholm's status as a world city necessitates a major emphasis on cybersecurity. Due to its growing reliance on technology, the city is at risk from cyberattacks that could interfere with crucial services, compromise private information, or even damage vital infrastructure. To protect the city's digital infrastructure and uphold the privacy and security of its residents, cooperation between government organizations, corporations, and cybersecurity professionals is essential.

Another important factor is the safety of public transit. The public transportation system in Stockholm, which includes buses, trains, and subways, is effective and vast. Passenger safety is enhanced by routine maintenance, severe safety inspections, and public awareness initiatives. To reduce panic and promote orderly reactions during emergencies, clearly established evacuation procedures and effective communication networks are crucial.

When visiting Stockholm, what to do and what not to do

Steps to Take:

Explore Gamla Stan: Begin your journey by taking a stroll around the historic streets of Gamla Stan.

The medieval structures and cobblestone streets provide a setting that transports you back in time.

Visit a Museum: Stockholm is home to a number of top-notch museums. The ABBA Museum honors the legendary musical trio, while the Vasa Museum displays a remarkable example of a battleship from the 17th century. With its engaging exhibits, the Fotografiska Museum draws photography enthusiasts.

Take Advantage of Nature: The city's unusual geography, which comprises 14 islands, provides a wealth of options to spend time outside. Visit the royal park Djurgrden for a leisurely stroll or take a boat tour to see the islands.

Try Swedish Cuisine: Snack on classic Swedish fare including gravlax, herring, and meatballs. Don't skip fika, a traditional coffee break with pastries.

Experience nighttime: Stockholm has a thriving and diversified nighttime scene. There is something for everyone, from hip bars and nightclubs to jazz salons and live music places.

What to Avoid:

Avoid Rush Hours: Stockholm can experience extremely congested times, particularly on public transportation. Avoid traveling as much as you can in the morning and evening rush hours.

Avoid skipping public transit because it is effective and well-connected in Stockholm. Use trams, buses, and the subway in addition to taxis to navigate around the city.

Swedish people appreciate their privacy and personal space. Even in crowded areas, it is best to keep your distance out of respect for the residents.

Follow Alcohol Regulations: Sweden has strict laws about alcohol. The legal drinking age is 18, and you can only purchase alcoholic beverages from state-owned Systembolaget establishments. Drinking in public is typically frowned upon.

Keep Cash on Hand: Despite Sweden's reputation for technological advancement, some smaller businesses may still prefer cash payments. Carrying a small quantity of local cash is a good idea.

Avoid Jaywalking: is frowned upon in Sweden, a country famed for its devotion to laws. Always cross the street at authorized crosswalks and wait for the green signal.

Chapter 7: being aware of foreign transaction fees

Understand the Policies of Your Card: Prior to your journey to Stockholm, it's important to be aware of the international transaction fees that may apply to your credit or debit card. To find out the particular charges your bank or credit card company levies for overseas transactions, get in touch with them. For specific transactions, some cards even forgo their fees.

Currency Conversion: If you use your card to make a purchase, you may have the option of paying in either your home currency or the local one (the Swedish Krona, SEK). To avoid dynamic currency conversion expenses, if the merchant's exchange rate might not be beneficial, choose the local currency.

Think About Travel-Friendly Cards: If you frequently travel abroad, it may be worthwhile to consider credit cards made with travelers in mind. These cards are a wise choice for your trip to Stockholm because they frequently include benefits like waived or reduced foreign transaction costs.

Utilizing prepaid travel cards is an additional choice for controlling foreign transaction fees. With these cards, you can load a certain sum of money onto the card in advance and use it much like a debit or credit card to make purchases. Prepaid cards can assist you in avoiding unforeseen expenses and frequently provide low exchange rates.

If you require cash, be advised that ATM withdrawals may potentially be subject to foreign transaction fees. The local ATM operator may charge you in addition to the cost levied by your home bank. Withdraw greater sums less frequently to reduce fees.

Inform Your Bank: Before leaving for Stockholm, let your bank know the dates and place of your trip. This lessens the chance that usage of your card overseas will raise a red alert about questionable conduct.

For fee-free or reduced-fee withdrawals, look for partner banks. Some banks have global alliances or partners that provide these services. To maximize your withdrawals, find out if your bank has Stockholm-based partner banks.

Avoiding cell phone roaming charges

When visiting Stockholm, avoiding cell phone roaming fees can help you spend less money and relax more. When you use your cell phone on a foreign network, roaming fees apply, incurring astronomical costs that can build up quickly. However, you may simply avoid these fees and stay connected without spending a fortune if you do a little forward planning and research on the local mobile market.

Consider buying a local SIM card first and foremost. Perhaps the best approach to prevent paying roaming fees is to do this. You may get a prepaid SIM card from a variety of carriers at the airport, electronics stores, or convenience stores all across the city after you arrive in Stockholm. You can stay connected at local prices with these SIM cards' built-in data, call, and text allowances. Just make sure your phone is unlocked and works with the frequencies used by the neighborhood networks.

Activating an international roaming plan with your home carrier is an additional choice. Even though there can still be some costs involved, they are usually less than the regular roaming rates. Before your travel, speak with your carrier to learn about the pricing and available options.

Using Wi-Fi networks is an excellent strategy to stay away from roaming fees. The technologically savvy city of Stockholm has a wide variety of free Wi-Fi sites available in cafés, restaurants, on public transportation, and even in certain outdoor areas. To reduce your reliance on mobile data, use Wi-Fi for data-intensive tasks like social networking, messaging, and surfing.

To interact with friends and family back home, think about using messaging apps that require an internet connection, like WhatsApp, Telegram, or Viber. With these apps, you may communicate with others via text messages, voice calls, and even the sharing of media.

preventing mobile roaming fees

When visiting Stockholm, avoiding cell phone roaming fees can help you spend less money and relax more. When you use your cell phone on a foreign network, roaming fees apply, incurring astronomical costs that can build up quickly. However, you may simply avoid these fees and stay connected without spending a fortune if you do a little forward planning and research on the local mobile market.

Consider buying a local SIM card first and foremost. Perhaps the best approach to prevent paying roaming fees is to do this. You may get a prepaid SIM card from a variety of carriers at the airport, electronics stores, or convenience stores all across the city after you arrive in Stockholm. You can stay connected at local prices with these SIM cards' built-in data, call, and text allowances. Just make sure your phone is unlocked and works with the frequencies used by the neighborhood networks.

Activating an international roaming plan with your home carrier is an additional choice. Even though there can still be some costs involved, they are usually less than the regular roaming rates. Before your travel, speak with your carrier to learn about the pricing and available options.

Using Wi-Fi networks is an excellent strategy to stay away from roaming fees. The technologically savvy city of Stockholm has a wide variety of free Wi-Fi sites available in cafés, restaurants, on public transportation, and even in certain outdoor areas. To reduce your reliance on mobile data, use Wi-Fi for data-intensive tasks like social networking, messaging, and surfing.

To interact with friends and family back home, think about using messaging apps that require an internet connection, like WhatsApp, Telegram, or Viber. With these apps, you may communicate with others via text messages, voice calls, and even the sharing of media.

Think of a Stockholm mobile phone or mifi

Staying connected while traveling is more important than ever in the hyperconnected world of today. Having a trustworthy communication tool is essential for all purposes, be they business-related, recreational, or simply keeping in touch with loved ones. The Stockholm cell phone and the MiFi device stand out as two popular options for maintaining constant contact while on the fly.

For people who prefer simplicity and functionality, the Stockholm cell phone is a flexible and practical option. The Stockholm cell phone, created with the modern traveler in mind, provides necessary communication tools without the distractions of a full-fledged smartphone. It allows for calling and messaging, guaranteeing that you may be reached wherever you are. The Stockholm cell phone is a dependable travel companion for people who wish to stay in touch without the weight and complexity of a smartphone thanks to its slim form and long battery life.

The MiFi device, on the other hand, offers a new method of mobile connectivity. A mobile hotspot called a MiFi, or "Mobile WiFi," enables a number of devices to access to the internet via a cellular data connection. For travelers who need internet connectivity for laptops, tablets, and other devices, this is the best option. You can work, browse, and interact with ease while on the go thanks to the

MiFi device's personal WiFi network. It is simple to carry in a pocket or purse due to its small size.

The decision between a Stockholm cell phone and a MiFi device ultimately comes down to your individual requirements and preferences. The Stockholm cell phone can be the best option if you value a simple communication tool. The MiFi device, however, might be the answer you're searching for if you need to connect many devices to the internet and retain a digital presence while traveling.

Obtain a map offline

For both visitors and locals, downloading an offline map of Stockholm can be a very useful resource. Sweden's capital, Stockholm, is well known for its stunning architecture, extensive history, and dynamic culture. Having an offline map makes for a seamless and stress-free trip, whether traveling through Gamla Stan, the city's picturesque old town, or taking in the numerous museums and attractions.

In a city like Stockholm, where internet may be spotty or expensive for foreign visitors, an offline map offers a number of benefits. Without relying on data or Wi-Fi connections, one can obtain important information via an offline map. This is especially helpful while using public transportation or strolling the city's confusing streets. The fear of being lost is eliminated and effective route planning is made possible by being able to pinpoint your precise location on an offline map.

Another place where offline maps excel is the archipelago of Stockholm, which consists of 14 islands connected by ferries and bridges. With a downloadable map, navigating the waterways to visit islands like Djurgrden or Gröna Lund becomes considerably simpler. It enables you to explore the city's numerous neighborhoods, each of which has a unique personality and attractions.

A sense of security is added by an offline map. Having a digital guide that doesn't rely on real-time connectivity in an unfamiliar environment ensures that you can always find your way back to your lodging or learn about nearby areas of interest.

The option to download Stockholm offline maps is available on many different apps and platforms. For instance, users of Google Maps can choose a specific location and save it for offline use. Offline maps with extra features like restaurant recommendations, directions to public transportation, and sightseeing ideas are also offered by other specialized travel apps.

An offline map is a necessary travel companion in a city like Stockholm, where fascinating discoveries are around every turn. It encourages deeper connections with the history and culture of the city and encourages exploration. Downloading an offline map of Stockholm is a simple but crucial step toward confidently and easily seeing the city's delights, whether you're a tech-savvy visitor or a local looking for convenience.

study a simple languages

A rewarding experience that opens doors to greater cultural immersion and meaningful connections is learning the fundamentals of the language in Stockholm. Despite the fact that English is widely spoken in this multicultural city, making the effort to learn a few simple Swedish words will tremendously improve your visit and help you make friends with locals.

Swedish is a fascinating language with its own distinctive charm, and even a basic grasp of it can be helpful. The Danish words "Hej" (hello) and "Tack" (thank you) can be used to make friends with locals. When you can speak in the local language, tasks like ordering dinner, shopping, and getting directions become more interesting.

The best approach to acquire the fundamentals of Swedish in Stockholm is through language exchange gatherings and classes. Numerous cultural institutions, civic associations, and language schools provide beginner-focused programs. These programs not only give structured instruction but also opportunity for practice with other students, giving you more confidence in practical settings.

Being fully immersed in the culture can also help you learn a language. You can gradually learn Swedish's rhythm and vocabulary by engaging in daily activities like reading menus, signs, and commercials in it. Speaking to locals in their language of origin demonstrates your respect for their culture and frequently inspires them to interact with you more amiably.

On this journey, technology is your friend. Apps and websites for language learning include interactive lessons and exercises that accommodate different learning styles. These tools provide you the flexibility to learn at your own pace and keep track of your development, assuring consistent advancement.

Additionally, finding conversation partners or groups can offer a more relaxed setting to practice speaking and listening skills. These encounters expose you to various accents and dialects while also providing insights into how informal language is used.

A doorway to a deeper understanding of the city and its residents can be opened by learning the fundamentals of Swedish in Stockholm. It shows that you are willing to engage with people on a deeper level, establishing a feeling of community and improving your experience in general. The benefits of being able to speak in the local tongue are tremendous, even though it could require some time and effort.

Airport cash is pricey

Travelers may find it very costly and inconvenient to exchange cash at the Stockholm airport. Sweden has adopted a cashless society and is renowned for its sophisticated digital infrastructure and wide acceptance of electronic payment systems. At the Stockholm airport, where cash purchases are frequently prohibited or subject to a surcharge, this trend is clearly visible.

Almost all of the airport's shops, eateries, and services are set up to accept card payments, whether they come in the form of a credit card, debit card, mobile payment app, or contactless payment. The country's commitment to sustainability is furthered by this efficiency, which not only expedites transactions but also reduces the need for physical currency and the related environmental costs.

Visitors and tourists who depend on cash might be at a disadvantage. In comparison to banks or other currency exchange services in the city, the exchange rates for currency conversion at the airport may be less beneficial. Due to the additional administrative work involved in handling and reconciling actual money, some stores may also add a service charge to cash transactions.

The best way to prepare for a trip to Stockholm is to have a compatible credit or debit card, a mobile payment app like Swish, or to make sure that your bank card can be used internationally. This strategy makes transactions easy not only at the airport but also throughout in the city, as card payments are commonly accepted in most businesses.

Conclusion

Embracing the City's Rich History and Culture

Stockholm, which is spread out over 14 islands at the meeting point of Lake Mälaren and the Baltic Sea, beckons visitors to immerse themselves in its rich tapestry of history and culture. Stockholm, the nation's capital, proudly displays a heritage that spans centuries, from its medieval beginnings to its allure today. Accepting the history of this city is more than just a choice; it's an invitation to embark on an enthralling trip through time.

Gamla Stan, the Old Town's cobblestone streets, wind through confined spaces dotted with vibrant structures, each of which has a unique tale to tell. Visitors can get lost here, following in the historical footsteps of kings, queens, and famous individuals. With its majestic appearance, the Royal Palace serves as a reminder of the city's monarchy and colorful past.

However, Stockholm's cultural attractions go beyond its old-world facades. The city hums with a thriving arts scene that includes theaters, galleries, and museums. The astoundingly well-preserved battleship from the 17th century is on display at the Vasa Museum, providing a window into Sweden's nautical past. The Fotografiska and Moderna Museet offer a contemporary alternative to the city's ancient sites for lovers of modern art and design.

Another entryway into Stockholm's culture is through its cuisine. The city's culinary scene, which ranges from traditional Swedish fare to foreign fusion, is a reflection of its multicultural nature. Visitors are immersed in a sensory experience where flavors, scents, and traditions collide when they explore local markets like stermalms saluhall.

Celebrations that honor both history and innovation are held around the city. Stockholm's events blend the ancient and the contemporary, showcasing the city's dynamic energy, from Midsummer celebrations that mark the summer solstice to the Nobel Prize ceremonies that honor ground-breaking accomplishments.

By embracing Stockholm's rich history and culture, one comes to understand a city where time is fluid, where the past shapes the present, and where a country's essence manifests itself in its customs, art, and architecture. The journey around Stockholm connects tourists with the heart of a vibrant, alive cultural history. It is more than just a physical experience.

Tips for solo travelers, family and LGBTQ+travelers

Advice for Various Travelers in Stockholm

The capital of Sweden, Stockholm, offers a distinctive fusion of old-world charm and cutting-edge innovation, making it a popular destination for LGBTQ+ visitors as well as families and solitary travelers. Here are some suggestions catered to each group's needs since each has its own interests and factors to take into account when exploring the city:

lone Adventurers: Stockholm provides a friendly and safe environment for lone travelers. For a more immersive experience, embrace the idea of "lagom," the Swedish notion of balance, and make an effort to fit in. Explore the picturesque ancient town of Gamla Stan and take advantage of the café scene.

Join a guided tour to meet other tourists and locals. A must-see attractions that offer chances to socialize with people while learning about Stockholm's history and popular culture are the Vasa Museum and the ABBA Museum.

Families: There are lots of family-friendly activities available in Stockholm for visitors of all ages. Children can learn about Swedish heritage and get to know native animals at Skansen, an outdoor museum and zoo. The Gröna Lund amusement park and Junibacken, a museum devoted to Astrid Lindgren's adored characters, are located on Djurgrden Island.

Kids will enjoy boating across the archipelago, so be sure to include boat rides in your agenda. Choose hotels with family-friendly features, and think about purchasing the Stockholm Pass for affordable access to several attractions.

Travelers who identify as LGBTQ+ should note that Stockholm is recognized for its welcoming environment. The Södermalm neighborhood has a thriving queer community with several bars, clubs, and events. Don't miss the annual spectacular honoring diversity that is the Stockholm Pride Festival.

Although Sweden is progressive, it's important to be aware that polite behavior in religious or traditional places is appreciated. Public demonstrations of affection are frequently acceptable. To get the most out of LGBTQ+-focused events and to get local insights, get in touch with LGBTQ+ groups or tour guides.

Whatever kind of traveler you are, Stockholm will entice you with its own personality and wide range of options. All while savoring the rich culture and breathtaking surroundings of this Scandinavian treasure, solo travelers can make connections, families can make enduring experiences, and LGBTQ+ visitors can embrace an open and welcoming society.

Printed in Great Britain
by Amazon